52 THINGS TO DO WHILE YOU POO
THE 1960s EDITION

AN HACHETTE UK COMPANY
WWW.HACHETTE.CO.UK

SUMMERSDALE PUBLISHERS LTD
PART OF OCTOPUS PUBLISHING GROUP LIMITED
CARMELITE HOUSE
50 VICTORIA EMBANKMENT
LONDON
EC4Y 0DZ
UK

WWW.SUMMERSDALE.COM
PRINTED AND BOUND IN CHINA
ISBN: 978-1-80007-431-6

SUBSTANTIAL DISCOUNTS ON BULK QUANTITIES OF SUMMERSDALE BOOKS
ARE AVAILABLE TO CORPORATIONS, PROFESSIONAL ASSOCIATIONS AND
OTHER ORGANIZATIONS. FOR DETAILS CONTACT GENERAL ENQUIRIES:
TELEPHONE: +44 (0) 1243 771107 OR EMAIL: ENQUIRIES@SUMMERSDALE.COM.

52 THINGS TO DO WHILE YOU POO

THE 1960s EDITION

HUGH JASSBURN

IF YOU GREW UP IN THE 1960s, YOU KNOW THAT NOTHING COMPARES TO THE MUSIC, FASHION, TOYS, TV, FILMS AND SHEER *FEEL* OF THAT DECADE. BUT HOW MUCH CAN YOU REALLY REMEMBER? WHEN YOU NEXT TAKE A TRIP TO THE TOILET, THIS COLOURFUL COLLECTION OF PUZZLES, ACTIVITIES AND TRIVIA WILL SERVE AS A LEISURELY STROLL DOWN MEMORY LANE, DUSTING OFF HALF-REMEMBERED FACTS AND EVEN FILLING IN A FEW GAPS.

THIS PAIR ONLY APPEARS ONCE
ON THE OPPOSITE PAGE

**A MINI WON THE MONTE CARLO RALLY IN
1964, 1965 AND 1967 BUT WAS DISQUALIFIED
AFTER ALSO FINISHING FIRST IN 1966. WHY?**

A) IT HAD ILLEGAL HEADLAMPS

B) THE DRIVER SWORE AT THE JUDGES

**C) IT WAS DRIVEN IN AN AGGRESSIVE
AND DANGEROUS MANNER**

THE BOUFFANT

THE BEEHIVE

THE FLICK-UP

THE PIXIE

THE AFRO

WHICH POPULAR 1960s HAIRSTYLE DID THE MODEL TWIGGY MAKE FAMOUS IN 1966?

52 THINGS TO DO WHILE YOU POO...

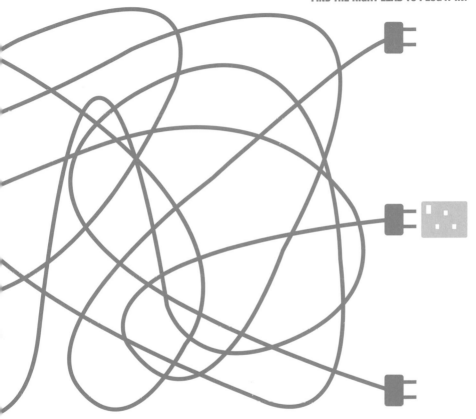

FIND THE RIGHT LEAD TO PLUG IT IN!

HOLYOAKE (KEITH, PRIME MINISTER, NEW ZEALAND, 60–72)

O'NEILL (TERENCE, PRIME MINISTER, NORTHERN IRELAND, 63–69)

LYNCH (JACK, TAOISEACH, REPUBLIC OF IRELAND, 66–73)

BREZHNEV (LEONID, GENERAL SECRETARY, SOVIET UNION, 64–82)

WILSON (HAROLD, PRIME MINISTER, UNITED KINGDOM, 64–70)

JOHNSON (LYNDON, PRESIDENT, UNITED STATES, 63–69)

KHAN (AYUB, PRESIDENT, PAKISTAN, 58–69)

HOLT (HAROLD, PRIME MINISTER, AUSTRALIA, 66–67)

PEARSON (LESTER BOWLES, PRIME MINISTER, CANADA, 63–68)

DE GAULLE (CHARLES, PRESIDENT, FRANCE, 59–69)

GANDHI (INDIRA, PRIME MINISTER, INDIA, 66–77)

M	N	B	N	V	C	Z	V	A	S
L	J	A	H	J	G	E	F	D	E
P	H	O	U	O	N	K	S	L	L
K	P	Y	T	H	R	A	E	Y	L
E	E	W	Z	N	K	O	N	N	U
R	A	E	T	S	Y	Y	O	C	A
P	R	O	I	O	U	L	S	H	G
B	S	B	N	N	H	O	L	T	E
K	O	G	A	N	D	H	I	B	D
O	N	E	I	L	L	H	W	M	J

PEOPLE TODAY ARE STILL LIVING OFF THE TABLE SCRAPS OF THE SIXTIES. THEY ARE STILL BEING PASSED AROUND – THE MUSIC AND THE IDEAS.

BOB DYLAN

IT'S JULY 1965, SO GET BOB TO NEWPORT FOLK FESTIVAL – HE'S GOING ELECTRIC!

TIDY UP THE TUNE TIMELINE – MATCH THE SONG TO THE YEAR IT WAS RELEASED

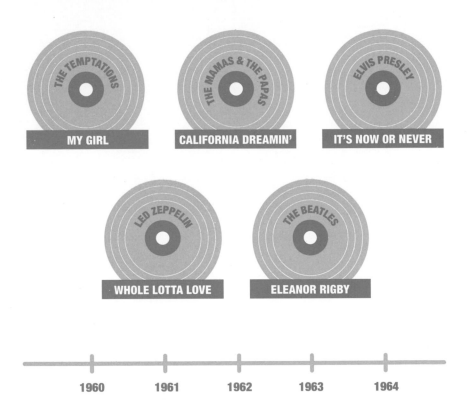

THE TEMPTATIONS
MY GIRL

THE MAMAS & THE PAPAS
CALIFORNIA DREAMIN'

ELVIS PRESLEY
IT'S NOW OR NEVER

LED ZEPPELIN
WHOLE LOTTA LOVE

THE BEATLES
ELEANOR RIGBY

1960   1961   1962   1963   1964

TWIST AND SHOUT

I'M WAITING FOR THE MAN

SYMPATHY FOR THE DEVIL

CRAZY

RING OF FIRE

1965   1966   1967   1968   1969

BRITISH SCI-FI TV SHOW *DOCTOR WHO* WAS FIRST BROADCAST IN 1963, BUT WHO PLAYED THE DOCTOR FROM OCTOBER 1966 UNTIL JUNE 1969?

A) WILLIAM HARTNELL

B) PATRICK TROUGHTON

C) TOM BAKER

WINKLE-PICKER SHOES WERE POPULAR IN THE 1960s WITH ROCK 'N' ROLL FANS. IN PARTS OF SCANDINAVIA THEY ARE CALLED "*MYGGJAGARE*". WHAT DOES THIS TRANSLATE TO?

A) MOSQUITO CHASERS

B) NOSE PICKERS

C) BOTTOM SCRATCHERS

EACH 2x2 BLOCK, COLUMN AND ROW SHOULD CONTAIN THE FOUR OBJECTS

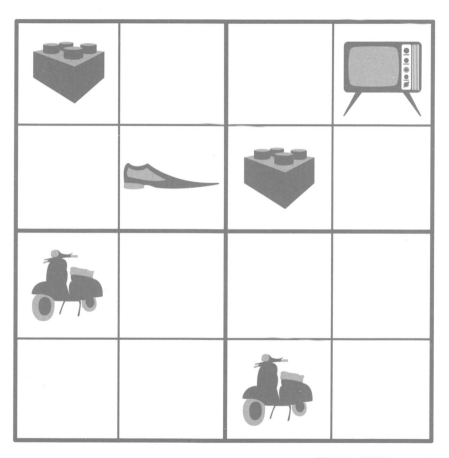

THIS PAIR ONLY APPEARS ONCE ON THE OPPOSITE PAGE

DURING THE 1960s, WHICH SUBCULTURE WAS ASSOCIATED WITH MOPEDS?

A) PUNKS

B) MODS

C) ROCKERS

IN THE MID-SIXTIES, THE COMPANY BEHIND THE POPULAR TOY MR POTATO HEAD LAUNCHED TWO NEW CHARACTERS TO JOIN HIM. WHAT WERE THEY CALLED?

A) ANNE THE AVO AND BEN THE BANANA

B) CLAIRE THE CUCUMBER AND ROBERT THE RADISH

C) OSCAR THE ORANGE AND PETE THE PEPPER

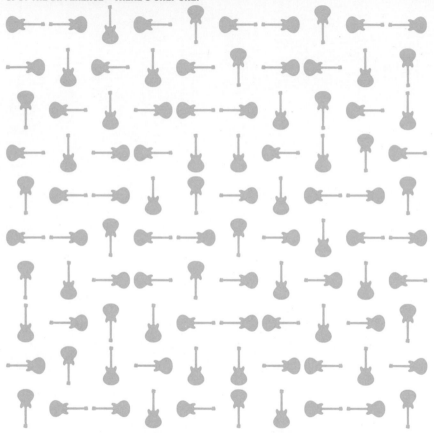

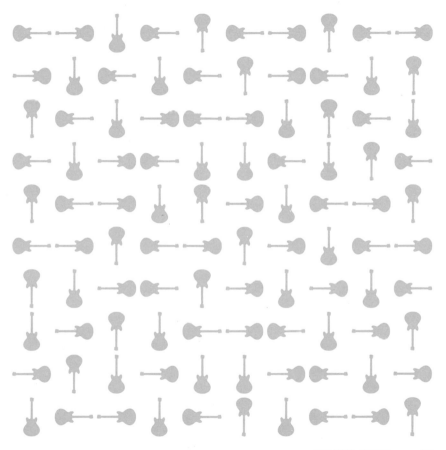

THE WHOLE 1960s THING WAS A TEN-YEAR RUNNING PARTY... IT STARTED AT THE END OF THE FIFTIES AND SORT OF FADED A BIT WHEN IT BECAME MUDDLED WITH FLOWER POWER. IT WAS MARVELLOUS.

MARY QUANT

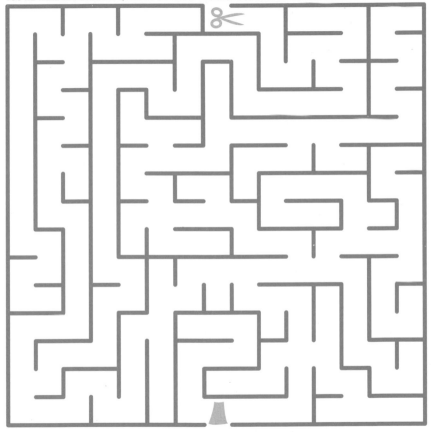

52 THINGS TO DO WHILE YOU POO...

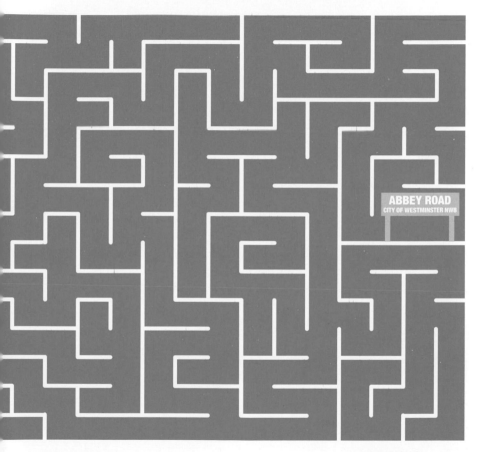

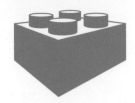

LEGO WAS FIRST SEEN IN BRITAIN AT THE BRIGHTON TOY FAIR IN 1960, BUT WHEN WAS LEGO'S LONDON BUS KIT INTRODUCED?

A) 1961

B) 1966

C) 1969

WHO INVENTED THE POPULAR 1960s DRAWING TOY ETCH A SKETCH?

A) AN AMATEUR MAGICIAN FROM THE USA

B) AN ELECTRICIAN FROM FRANCE

C) A STONE MASON FROM BRITAIN

BONO (10 MAY 1960)

MINOGUE (KYLIE, 28 MAY 1968)

MARADONA (DIEGO, 30 OCTOBER 1960)

OBAMA (BARACK, 4 AUGUST 1961)

DION (CELINE, 30 MARCH 1968)

SPENCER (DIANA, 1 JULY 1961)

TARANTINO (QUENTIN, 27 MARCH 1963)

ROWLING (J. K., 31 JULY 1965)

RAMSAY (GORDON, 8 NOVEMBER 1966)

CRAWFORD (CINDY, 20 FEBRUARY 1966)

W	S	P	E	N	C	E	R	W	E
R	I	U	Y	T	O	T	O	R	D
T	A	R	A	N	T	I	N	O	R
E	N	R	A	P	O	N	D	W	O
B	O	N	O	M	J	P	G	L	F
G	D	L	B	G	S	R	D	I	W
Y	A	E	A	W	J	A	L	N	A
T	R	U	M	I	O	P	Y	G	R
E	A	W	A	A	S	D	F	G	C
R	M	I	N	O	G	U	E	H	J

PROTEST PEACEFULLY –
FIND THE "FLOWER POWER" FLOWER

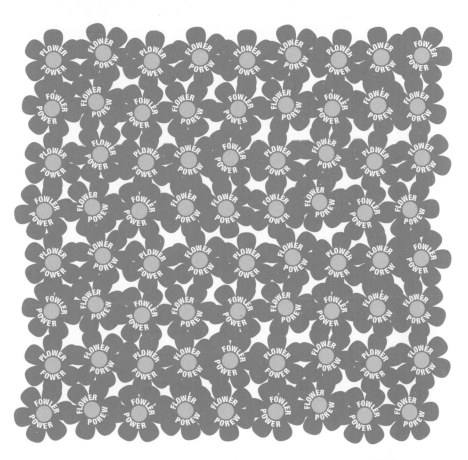

EACH 2x2 BLOCK, COLUMN AND ROW SHOULD CONTAIN THE FOUR 1960s PARTY FAVOURITES

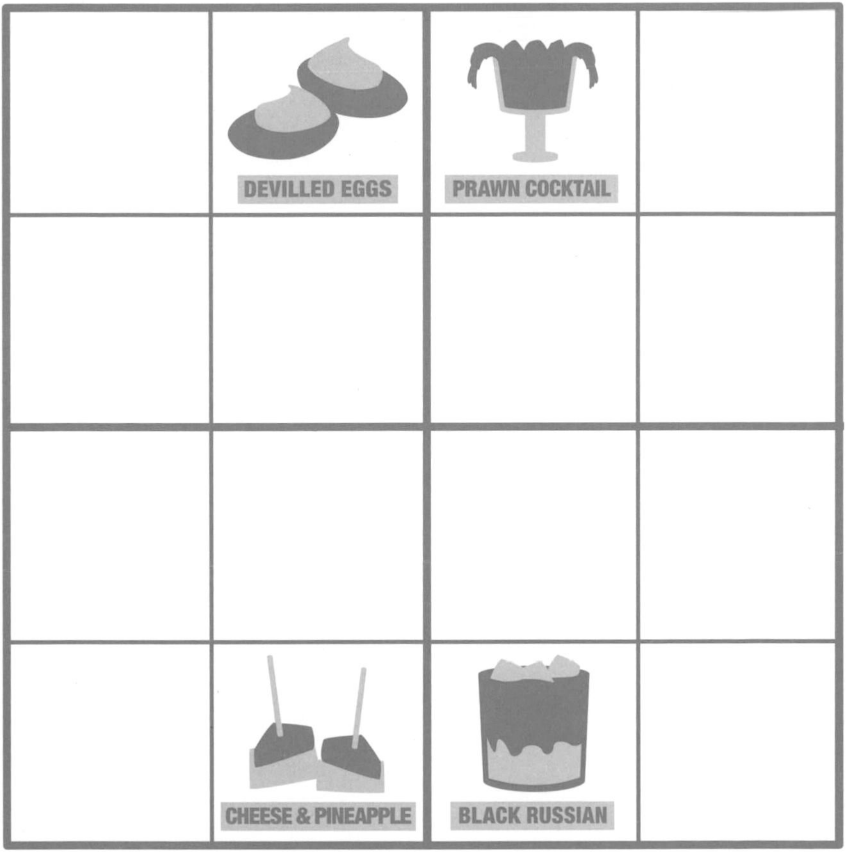

DEVILLED EGGS

PRAWN COCKTAIL

CHEESE & PINEAPPLE

BLACK RUSSIAN

COURAGE IS BEING SCARED TO DEATH... AND SADDLING UP ANYWAY.

JOHN WAYNE

IT'S 1969, SO GET JOHN TO HIS HORSE – HE NEEDS TO FILM *TRUE GRIT*!

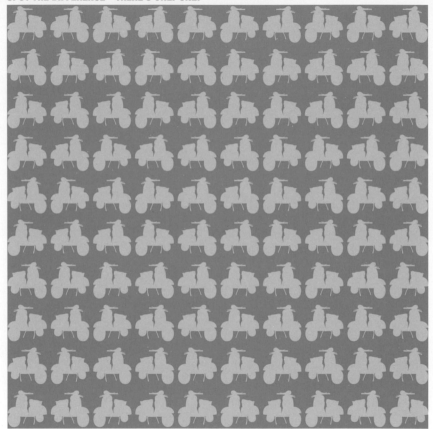

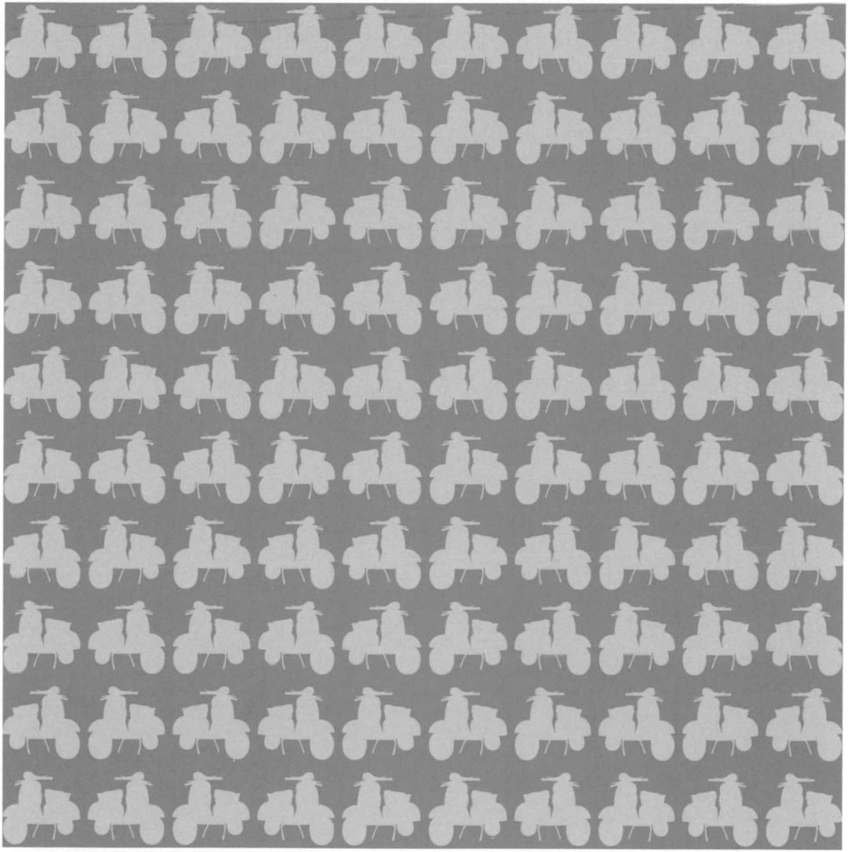

THIS PAIR ONLY APPEARS ONCE
ON THE OPPOSITE PAGE

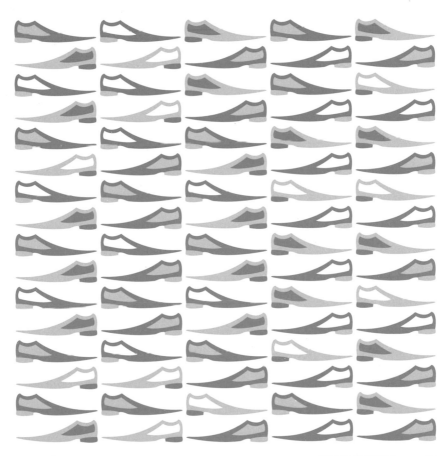

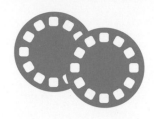

**IN 1962, VIEW-MASTER LAUNCHED
THE MODEL G, MADE FROM A NEW, LIGHTER
PLASTIC TO HOLD THE REELS. HOW MANY
SCENES WERE IN THESE REELS?**

A) 9

B) 8

C) 7

WHICH JAMES BOND FILM APPEARED IN UK CINEMAS IN 1962 AND US CINEMAS IN 1963?

A) *FROM RUSSIA WITH LOVE*

B) *THUNDERBALL*

C) *DR. NO*

GET YOUR CRAYONS OUT

COLOUR THE FLOWER
(IN 1960s COLOURS)

A PUNK HAS STOLEN A MOPED! FIND THEM!

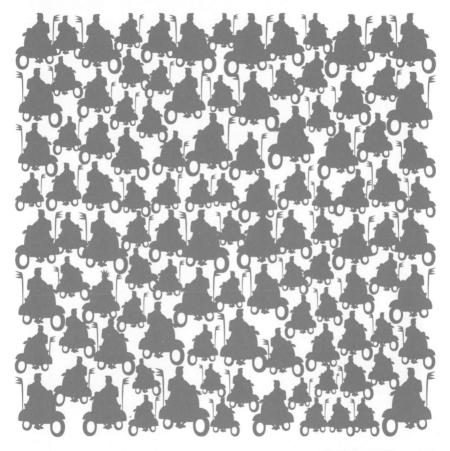

THAT'S ONE SMALL STEP FOR MAN, ONE GIANT LEAP FOR MANKIND.

NEIL ARMSTRONG

BEFORE BEING KNOWN AS THE BEACH BOYS, WHAT NAME DID THE BAND USE?

A) THE FINS

B) THE SURFERS

C) THE PENDLETONES

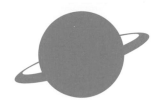

***STAR TREK*, SET IN THE TWENTY-THIRD CENTURY, DEBUTED ON 8 SEPTEMBER 1966. IT FOLLOWED THE ADVENTURES OF A SPACE EXPLORATION VESSEL BUILT BY WHICH BODY?**

A) THE UNIFIED UNIVERSE ESTABLISHMENT

B) THE PLANET POWER AUTHORITY

C) THE UNITED FEDERATION OF PLANETS

SPOT THE DIFFERENCE – THERE'S ONLY ONE!

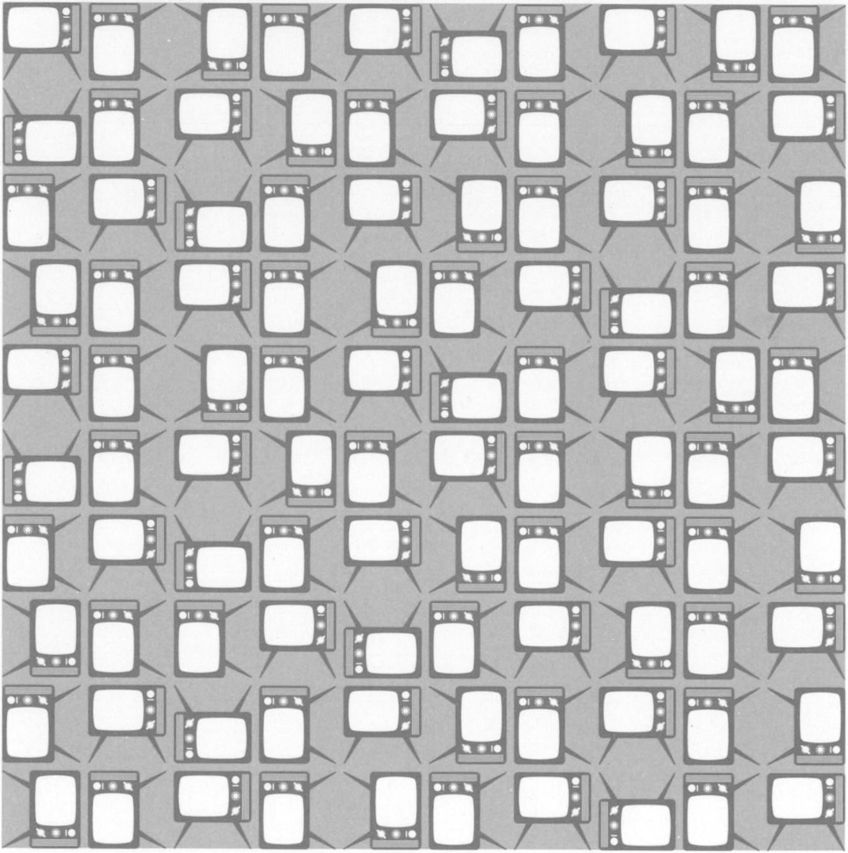

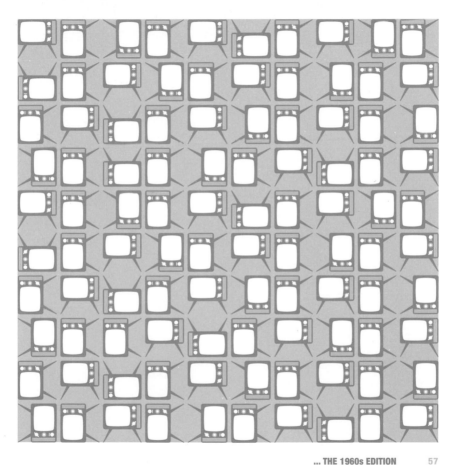

THIS PAIR ONLY APPEARS ONCE
ON THE OPPOSITE PAGE

WAYNE (JOHN)

ANDREWS (JULIE)

NEWMAN (PAUL)

CONNERY (SEAN)

BURTON (RICHARD)

SHARIF (OMAR)

CHRISTIE (JULIE)

MARTIN (DEAN)

MacLAINE (SHIRLEY)

REDGRAVE (VANESSA)

R E D G R A V E M I
S I O B P L K M A U
W T F G U H A J C Y
E S D S A R C V L T
R I A M T N T B A R
D R D I Y J R O I E
N H N N E W M A N E
A C O N N E R Y E W
R E D G S H A R I F
A N D R H W G F G L

FIND THE POTATO TWIN!

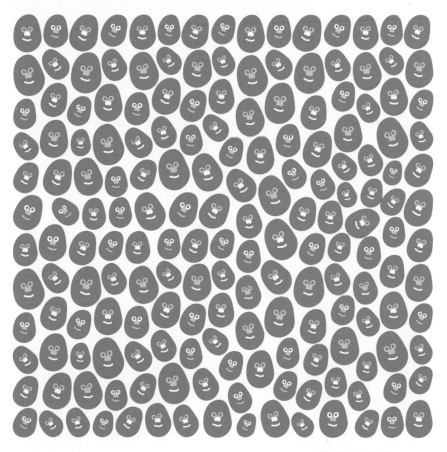

PARTY LIKE IT'S 1969

PARTY LIKE IT'S 1969

ON 28 AUGUST 1963, MARTIN LUTHER KING JR GAVE HIS "I HAVE A DREAM" SPEECH. WHERE IN WASHINGTON WAS HE?

A) OUTSIDE THE CAPITOL BUILDING

B) ON THE STEPS OF THE LINCOLN MEMORIAL

C) NEXT TO THE WASHINGTON MONUMENT

WHAT ARE THE THREE MAIN INGREDIENTS OF THE POPULAR 1960s DESSERT BAKED ALASKA?

A) ICE CREAM, CAKE AND MERINGUE

B) CUSTARD, CAKE AND MERINGUE

C) ICE CREAM, BREAD AND MERINGUE

EACH 2x2 BLOCK, COLUMN AND ROW SHOULD CONTAIN THE FOUR 1960s HAIRSTYLES

THE BOUFFANT

THE BEEHIVE

THE AFRO

THE FLICK-UP

IT'S 8.30 A.M. ON MONDAY 18 AUGUST 1969.
**JIMI HENDRIX IS ABOUT TO GO ON STAGE
AT WOODSTOCK BUT HE'S LOST HIS
ELECTRIC GUITAR – HELP HIM FIND IT!**

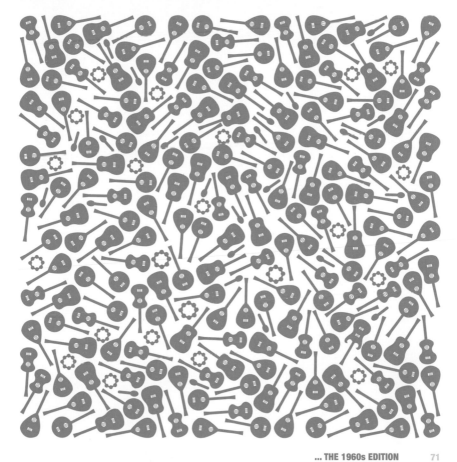

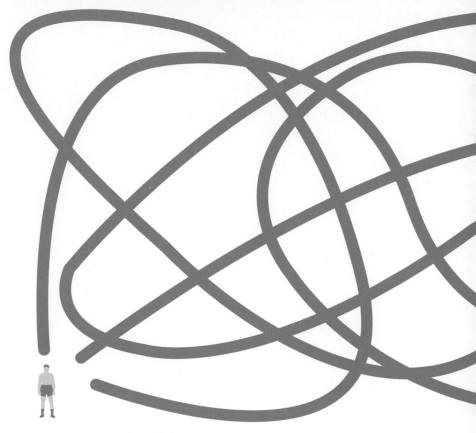

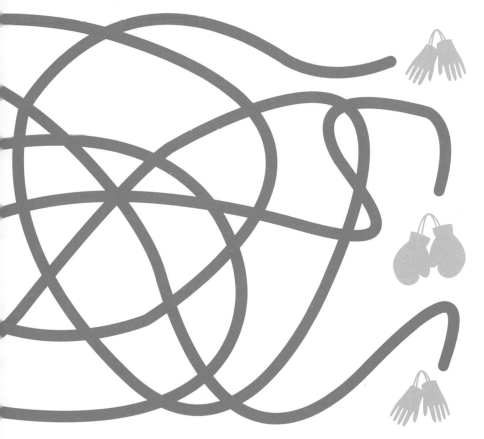

IN THE 1960s WHEN
THE RECORDING STUDIO...
TOOK OFF AS A TOOL, IT WAS THE
KIDS FROM ART SCHOOL WHO
KNEW HOW TO USE IT, NOT THE
KIDS FROM MUSIC SCHOOL.

BRIAN ENO

IT'S 1969 – GET BRIAN TO LONDON TO START HIS MUSIC CAREER

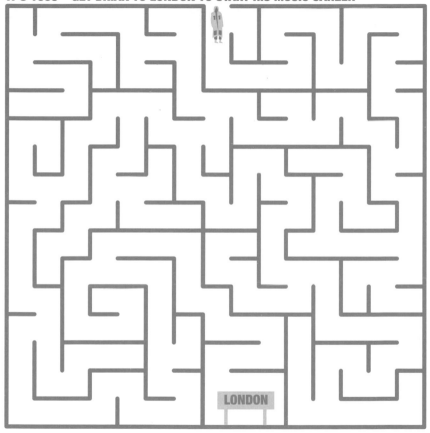

LONDON

THESE PEOPLE DIED IN THE 1960s – CAN YOU WORK OUT WHO DIED WHERE? ONE'S BEEN DONE FOR YOU

1960 **LOS ANGELES, USA**
1962 **LOS ANGELES, USA**
1962 **NEW YORK, USA**
1963 **OXFORD, ENGLAND**
1963 **VATICAN CITY**
1964 **CANTERBURY, ENGLAND**
1965 **SANTA MONICA, USA**
1965 **KENSINGTON, ENGLAND**
1966 **BURBANK, USA**
1967 **VALLEGRANDE, BOLIVIA**
1968 **HAMPSTEAD, ENGLAND**
1969 **LONDON, ENGLAND**
1969 **HANOI, NORTH VIETNAM**

POPE JOHN XXIII
RELIGIOUS LEADER

CHE GUEVARA
REVOLUTIONARY LEADER

CLARK GABLE
ACTOR

STAN LAUREL
ACTOR

JUDY GARLAND
ACTRESS

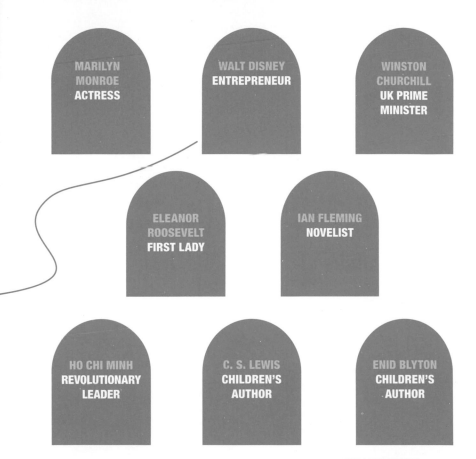

MARILYN
MONROE
ACTRESS

WALT DISNEY
ENTREPRENEUR

WINSTON
CHURCHILL
**UK PRIME
MINISTER**

ELEANOR
ROOSEVELT
FIRST LADY

IAN FLEMING
NOVELIST

HO CHI MINH
**REVOLUTIONARY
LEADER**

C. S. LEWIS
**CHILDREN'S
AUTHOR**

ENID BLYTON
**CHILDREN'S
AUTHOR**

WHICH BAND MADE THEIR DEBUT AT THE MARQUEE CLUB, LONDON, IN 1962?

A) THE ROLLING STONES

B) THE WHO

C) THE KINKS

WHICH ROALD DAHL BOOK WAS PUBLISHED IN JANUARY 1964 IN THE USA AND NOVEMBER 1964 IN THE UK?

A) *THE BFG*

B) *CHARLIE AND THE CHOCOLATE FACTORY*

C) *JAMES AND THE GIANT PEACH*

THIS PAIR ONLY APPEARS ONCE
ON THE OPPOSITE PAGE

BEATLES (THE)

BROWN (JAMES)

BEACH BOYS (THE)

DYLAN (BOB)

STONES (THE ROLLING)

SUPREMES (THE)

FRANKLIN (ARETHA)

PRESLEY (ELVIS)

COOKE (SAM)

HENDRIX (JIMI)

H	W	Y	M	N	C	O	U	T	B
E	F	R	A	N	K	L	I	N	E
N	E	R	B	R	O	W	N	H	A
D	P	N	T	E	N	N	S	G	C
R	O	I	K	K	A	E	X	F	H
I	W	O	J	L	N	T	A	D	B
X	O	G	Y	O	L	B	L	S	O
C	W	D	T	H	M	V	C	E	Y
M	S	S	U	P	R	E	M	E	S
D	F	G	P	R	E	S	L	E	Y

WHAT SORT OF FAMILY TIE DID GREGORY PECK HAVE WITH THE 1968 FILM *THE BIG COUNTRY*?

A) HIS MOTHER PLAYED THE ROLE OF HIS MOTHER

B) HE APPEARED WITH HIS THREE SONS

C) HIS BROTHER PLAYED THE ROLE OF HIS BROTHER

WHICH COUNTRY INAUGURATED A NEW FLAG IN A PUBLIC CEREMONY ON 15 FEBRUARY 1965?

A) CANADA

B) CONGO

C) FIJI

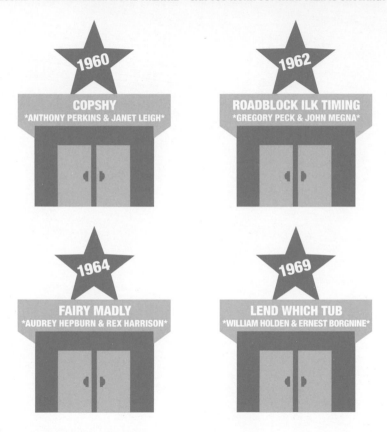

1960
COPSHY
ANTHONY PERKINS & JANET LEIGH

1962
ROADBLOCK ILK TIMING
GREGORY PECK & JOHN MEGNA

1964
FAIRY MADLY
AUDREY HEPBURN & REX HARRISON

1969
LEND WHICH TUB
WILLIAM HOLDEN & ERNEST BORGNINE

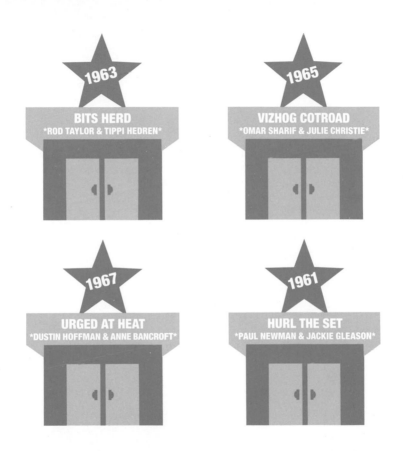

1963

BITS HERD
ROD TAYLOR & TIPPI HEDREN

1965

VIZHOG COTROAD
OMAR SHARIF & JULIE CHRISTIE

1967

URGED AT HEAT
DUSTIN HOFFMAN & ANNE BANCROFT

1961

HURL THE SET
PAUL NEWMAN & JACKIE GLEASON

FIND 1960

```
1 6 9 0 1 0 9 6 1 6 0 6 1 9 6 9 1 6 0 6
6 1 6 9 0 1 0 9 6 1 6 0 6 1 9 6 9 1 6 0
0 6 1 9 6 9 1 6 0 6 1 6 9 0 1 0 9 6 1 6
6 0 6 1 6 9 0 1 0 9 6 1 6 0 6 1 0 6 9 1
6 1 6 9 0 1 0 9 6 1 6 0 6 1 9 6 9 1 6 0
1 6 9 0 1 0 9 6 1 6 0 6 1 9 6 9 1 6 0 6
6 0 6 1 6 9 0 1 0 9 6 1 6 0 6 1 9 6 9 1
1 6 0 6 1 6 9 0 1 0 9 6 1 6 0 6 1 9 6 9
6 9 0 1 0 9 6 1 6 0 6 1 9 6 9 1 6 0 6 1
1 6 9 0 1 0 9 6 1 6 0 6 1 9 6 9 1 6 0 6
6 1 9 6 9 1 6 0 6 1 6 9 0 1 0 9 6 1 6 0
0 6 1 6 9 0 1 0 9 6 1 6 0 6 1 9 6 9 1 6
1 6 9 0 1 0 9 6 1 6 0 6 1 9 6 9 1 6 0 6
6 9 0 1 0 9 6 1 6 0 6 1 9 6 9 1 6 0 6 1
0 6 1 6 9 0 1 0 9 6 1 6 0 6 1 9 6 9 1 6
6 0 6 1 6 9 0 1 0 9 6 1 6 0 6 1 9 6 9 1
6 9 0 1 9 6 0 1 6 0 6 1 9 6 9 1 6 0 6 1
9 0 1 0 9 6 1 6 0 6 1 9 6 9 1 6 0 6 1 6
6 1 6 9 0 1 0 9 6 1 6 0 6 1 9 6 9 1 6 0
0 6 1 6 9 0 1 0 9 6 1 6 0 6 1 9 6 9 1 6
```

THE FIRST TELEVISED AMERICAN PRESIDENTIAL DEBATE WAS HELD ON 26 SEPTEMBER 1960. WHO TOOK PART?

A) DWIGHT D. EISENHOWER AND JOHN F. KENNEDY

B) JOHN F. KENNEDY AND RICHARD M. NIXON

C) RICHARD M. NIXON AND DWIGHT D. EISENHOWER

THE GREAT TRAIN ROBBERY TOOK PLACE ON 8 AUGUST 1963 WITH £2.6 MILLION BEING STOLEN FROM A ROYAL MAIL TRAIN. WHERE WAS THE TRAIN HEADING?

A) FROM LONDON TO BIRMINGHAM

B) FROM GLASGOW TO LONDON

C) FROM LONDON TO CARDIFF

EACH 2x2 BLOCK, COLUMN AND ROW SHOULD CONTAIN THE FOUR 1960s TOYS

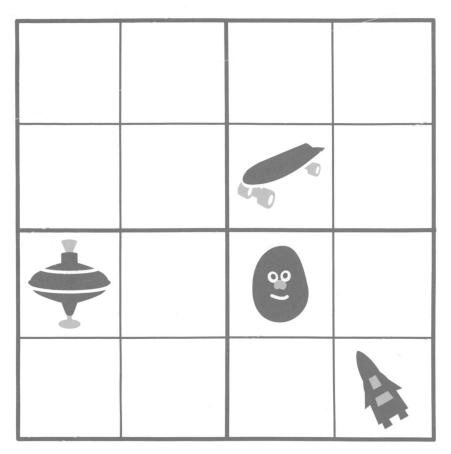

**THE FIRST PAIR OF UK DR. MARTENS
BOOTS ROLLED OFF THE PRODUCTION
LINE IN APRIL 1960. WHAT WAS
THE STYLE KNOWN AS?**

A) STYLE 1960

B) STYLE 1460

C) STYLE 1640

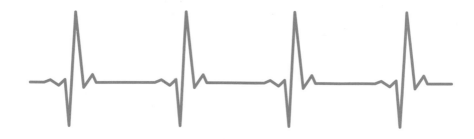

**ON THE 3 DECEMBER 1967,
THE WORLD'S FIRST HUMAN-TO-HUMAN
HEART TRANSPLANT WAS PERFORMED.
WHERE DID THIS TAKE PLACE?**

A) TOKYO, JAPAN

B) SYDNEY, AUSTRALIA

C) CAPE TOWN, SOUTH AFRICA

IT'S ANAGRAM TV FROM THE 1960s – CAN YOU WORK OUT WHAT'S ON?

EBB HELLISH LIVELY LITER
BIT CHEWED
HADDOCK EVE WHY STINK
NETTLES SHIFT NO
HEAVER GENTS

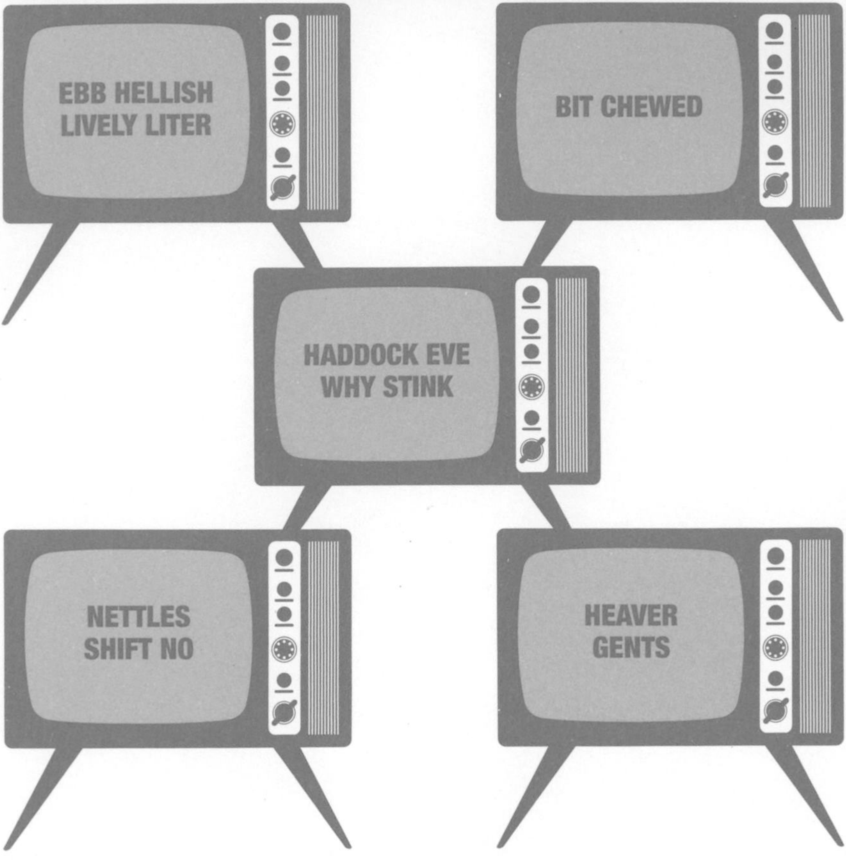

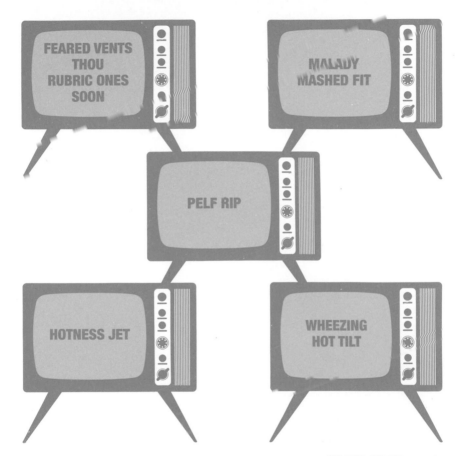

FEARED VENTS THOU RUBRIC ONES SOON

MALADY MASHED FIT

PELF RIP

HOTNESS JET

WHEEZING HOT TILT

ANSWERS

P6–7

P12–13

P8 A) IT HAD ILLEGAL HEADLAMPS
P9 THE PIXIE
P10–11

P15

P18 **B) PATRICK TROUGHTON**
P19 **A) MOSQUITO CHASERS**
P20–21

P16–17

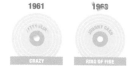

P22–23

P29

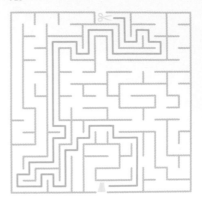

P24 B) MODS
P25 C) OSCAR THE ORANGE AND PETE THE PEPPER
P26–27

52 THINGS TO DO WHILE YOU POO...

P30–31

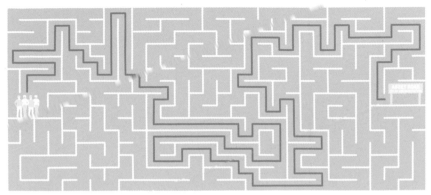

P32 B) 1966
P33 B) AN ELECTRICIAN FROM FRANCE
P34–35

P36–37

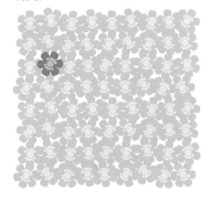

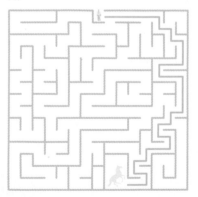

52 THINGS TO DO WHILE YOU POO...

P46 C) 7
P47 C) *DR. NO*
P50–51

P54 C) THE PENDLETONES
P55 C) THE UNITED FEDERATION OF PLANETS
P56–57

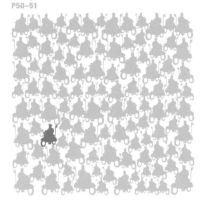

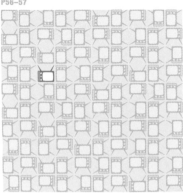

P53

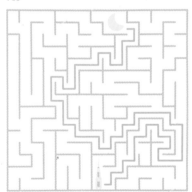

P58–59

P60–61

P64–65

PARTY LIKE IT'S 1969

P66 B) ON THE STEPS OF THE LINCOLN MEMORIAL
P67 A) ICE CREAM, CAKE AND MERINGUE
P68–69

P62–63

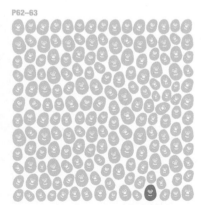

52 THINGS TO DO WHILE YOU POO...

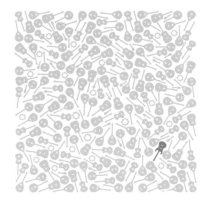

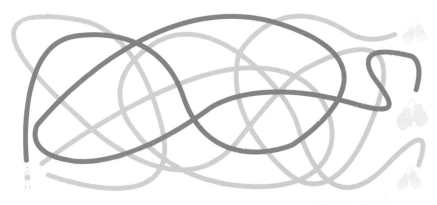

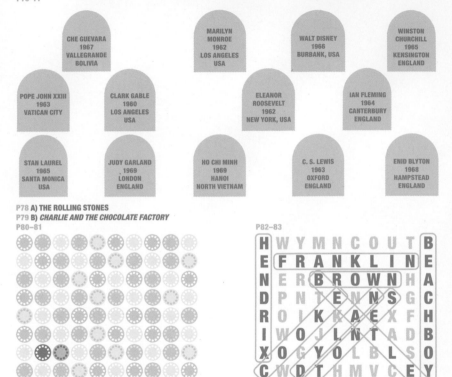

CHE GUEVARA
1967
VALLEGRANDE
BOLIVIA

MARILYN MONROE
1962
LOS ANGELES
USA

WALT DISNEY
1966
BURBANK, USA

WINSTON CHURCHILL
1965
KENSINGTON
ENGLAND

POPE JOHN XXIII
1963
VATICAN CITY

CLARK GABLE
1960
LOS ANGELES
USA

ELEANOR ROOSEVELT
1962
NEW YORK, USA

IAN FLEMING
1964
CANTERBURY
ENGLAND

STAN LAUREL
1965
SANTA MONICA
USA

JUDY GARLAND
1969
LONDON
ENGLAND

HO CHI MINH
1969
HANOI
NORTH VIETNAM

C. S. LEWIS
1963
OXFORD
ENGLAND

ENID BLYTON
1968
HAMPSTEAD
ENGLAND

P78 A) THE ROLLING STONES
P79 B) *CHARLIE AND THE CHOCOLATE FACTORY*
P80–81

P82–83

P84 **B) HE APPEARED WITH HIS THREE SONS**
P85 **A) CANADA**
P86–87

P88–89

```
1 6 9 0 1 0 9 6 1 6 0 6 1 9 6 9 1 6 0 6
6 1 6 9 0 1 0 9 6 1 6 0 6 1 9 6 9 1 6 0
0 6 1 9 6 9 1 6 0 6 1 6 9 0 1 0 9 6 1 6
6 0 6 1 6 9 0 1 0 9 6 1 6 0 6 1 0 6 9 1
6 1 6 9 0 1 0 9 6 1 6 0 6 1 9 6 9 1 6 0
1 6 9 0 1 0 9 6 1 6 0 6 1 9 6 9 1 6 0 6
6 0 6 1 6 9 0 1 0 9 6 1 6 0 6 1 9 6 9 1
1 6 0 6 1 6 9 0 1 0 9 6 1 6 0 6 1 9 6 9
6 9 0 1 0 9 6 1 6 0 6 1 9 6 9 1 6 0 6 1
1 6 9 0 1 0 9 6 1 6 0 6 1 9 6 9 1 6 0 6
6 1 9 6 9 1 6 0 6 1 9 6 9 0 1 0 9 6 1 6
0 6 1 6 9 0 1 0 9 6 1 6 0 6 1 9 6 9 1 6
1 6 9 0 1 0 9 6 1 6 0 6 1 9 6 9 1 6 0 6
6 9 0 1 0 9 6 1 6 0 6 1 9 6 9 1 6 0 6 1
0 6 1 6 9 0 1 0 9 6 1 6 0 6 1 9 6 3 1 6
6 0 6 1 6 9 0 1 0 9 6 1 6 0 0 1 9 6 9 1
6 9 0 1 1 9 6 0 1 6 0 6 1 9 6 9 1 6 0 6
9 0 1 0 9 6 1 6 0 0 1 9 6 9 1 6 0 6 1 6
6 1 6 9 0 1 0 9 6 1 6 0 6 1 9 6 9 1 6 0
0 6 1 0 9 0 1 0 9 6 1 6 0 6 1 9 6 0 1 6
```

P90–91

P92 B) JOHN F. KENNEDY AND RICHARD M. NIXON
P93 B) FROM GLASGOW TO LONDON
P94–95

P96 B) STYLE 1460
P97 C) CAPE TOWN, SOUTH AFRICA
P98–99

110   52 THINGS TO DO WHILE YOU POO...

HAVE YOU ENJOYED THIS BOOK? IF SO, FIND US ON FACEBOOK AT SUMMERSDALE PUBLISHERS, ON TWITTER AT @SUMMERSDALE AND ON INSTAGRAM AT @SUMMERSDALEBOOKS AND GET IN TOUCH. WE'D LOVE TO HEAR FROM YOU!

WWW.SUMMERSDALE.COM